MOTES

Well mote yee thee, as well can wish your thought.
                                          —Edmund Spenser

MOTES
Craig Dworkin

ROOF BOOKS
NEW YORK

To Mike &
For Miles

With special thanks to Sandra Doller, Rob Fitterman,
Judith Goldman, Bob Grenier, and Mónica de la Torre.

 This book was made possible, in part, with public funds from the New York
State Council on the Arts, a state agency.
NYSCA

Roof Books are distributed by
Small Press Distribution
1341 Seventh Street
Berkeley, CA. 94710-1403
Phone orders: 800-869-7553
www.spdbooks.org

Roof Books are published by
Segue Foundation
300 Bowery
New York, NY 10012
seguefoundation.com

CONTENTS

OPUSCULA

Opuscule, a little work, a little labor.
—Thomas Blount, *Glossographia* (1656)

A SHIVER

winters itself

LA SORBONNE

a winter city day

all marbled halls

CHEZ PORT ROYAL

shape suggests the golden age of large door panel depiction

CHARDIN

chagrin of plants
in natures mortes

FLÂNEUR

you astonish them;

they become regret

BRANCHED TREES

very trendy in these streets of steady arbitrary breezing

PARIS TRAIN STATION

hoping for more ostentatious decoration

PLEADING FOR A FEW CHURLS

I speak of the skirts of Arles

MASS OF TICKETS

mass of tickets bit
by the conductor's munching punch

JEUNE HOMME TRISTE DANS UN TRAIN

in marcel duchamp's sad young man on a train I am that man

THE THEORY OF INTUITION IN HUSSERL'S PHILOSOPHY

in your hand
you have
the wine

REMEMBERING LAST TIME

forgetting to order the duck oat stew szechuan

MY PANCAKES MY YOGURTS MY BISCUITS

when I touch it

SLUGGISH MILK

ugly really

ORNERY FLAG

well we know the sound of his toadying soap soft going

TOO MUCH LATHER ON

term of dry skin tomorrow

GENTAL

gumming

gones

purgatory diagnostics

HUSKY

plush

NOSTALGIA

we pain you,
disappearing
all the more

CATCHES OF SPRAIN

I ran a ways together, walking the road we go

SAFETY FIRST

brief fast has made me dangerously thirsty for juice

THIRSTY

for four days later

METAPHOR

the light above

the mossy rocks

VARIABLES

hob
peel

nept

WITHING

dright of shrinking insides

fissile meatloaf tinder

SEA SICK

too much marmalade now
starting to turn green

ROWDY LOUD LOCALS

rout of louts by dint of low clouds all around

DREGS OF THE LEASE

final deposits less my month

THUNDERCLOUDS

clearly loud under there

BRICK

Buick

IF FIVE GRAMS

took up costal agon

KARAOKE

singings a-
long to her
name is Rio
and

CELLO

ellipse

TOTALLY SOLD OUT

empty metal concession stands

about the one thing I wasn't sure about

JUST CAR ALARMS

whistling in the dark along without a cause

WHY

why such a warm sound from the far room
when the hum of the old mercedes comes
around again the block in summer humming

strung-out on cordials

LES SCHWAB TIRES

you shoot the Schwabs

STOP CASTING POROSITY

right this very minute

BERKELEY MARINA

frottage of fish grotto signage as
announcing the decline of the west

ORGY

open

roti

goat

jerk

BAD WESTERN

freak injury from cattle teeth

TOUGHS

legacy of calves grazing against the wire fences there

FROZEN PEACHES

conned by further hectoring american barricade lectures

CONNED BY FAKE FARM RECEIPT

endless stories about militant wheat

SHE'S A FOUNTAIN

trumpeting around the spray
that way behind the curtain

honking and donkeying about

CONSTANT DOMESTIC CHAOS

steady mestive swells of chest spasm bubble

CAR HORNS

core of wrenchèd chaos

THE BRONX

I brought the bought wooden box from there

CISTUS

citrus

OR

issue
waned

WOOL CABIN

we've been cool all winter

GOOD-BYE WINTER

no sled and no
snow

Frank Zappa

Franz Kafka

Die Walküre, die.

FOR THE WIDER GOOD

I am tiger woods

I am tiger woods

ANKLE OF LAWN

laws of perspective for foothills as was seen from above

FIND MY BEARINGS

I'll ask and see

APACHE

apace

ACQUISITION OF LANGUISH

foreign part-
iculates stag
-nated on thy
tongue

REMNANTS

of cuddle on the couch

STRONG PUB ACCENT

broken curlicue up
above the oaken or
nate bar ascending

two cute putti put
my tooth on edge

NAPPING

drooling off and on for almost twelve hours

OLD ANGEL

of yawn

SAINT AGNES

hands return to window silt

Godiva, go.

LAVISH VIZSLAS

obeying the leash laws

HYSTERIA

his stereo

its very own

finely wound

sounded room

WACK-A-MOLE

guacamole

walk a crooked mile

THE GOODS

lesbians every
couple of year

ANNOYS

allowed to continue

MILLING

workers circling
around the fact-
ory floor frowning

LITTLE WOMEN

increasing frown lines

SCEPTICAL SOUR POUT

that unconvincing faux suede purse was made
of mohair, as they say, which is to die for

DARFUR

hens

FREE REIGN

no refrain from singing around here

AN EGG

flash of white ab
-ove bikini domed

TWO BLUE BASSINETS

these five robins egg sinks here
below the trace of baby's-breath
sprigged in a bloom upon a fount

STILL ANOTHER CLEAN BREAK

poor paul celan such
easily broken bones

MARGIN

explanation of butter on the counter overnight

AN OUNCE

of ocean all at once
publishing in my eye

CAUGHT OUT

no drought

of draught

ITCHING

to change this book

FAT ALBERT

lemon yellow pee

JUNE SEPIA

I guess I don't know how old that old photo really is

JULY, AUGUST

ugly jelly sandwiches brighter now in the breeze

AFTER AN AFTERNOON NAP

yes, this

remaining

TO WARM THIS VIEW

Cuernavaca, Cuernavaca

FAIRER JACKET

sunny lemon tea time

some gold saw me
some gold saw me

AYRES

ayres of heuen blys.
—John Audelay

DOCKS

floating in a line on the water in the light

runks

AYRES

no worse for the cost of bird song answering the surf

AVES

hand clasped raised and talented askew
by her angular byzantined visage winks

SPANISH PULPIT

intolerant call for the expulsion of the jews from there

WILTED TULIPS

split little puppet pulpits tilted spilling dew

WINTER WARMING

knees now in range of that open
oven often after evening orange

WOODS

thick carpet of leaves would be so
good for slipping if you're a deer

APLOMB

bursts of a cold suite of puff-ruffled pur-
ple feathers in the furze among the plums

OUT OF RANGE TO HAIL

can't make out the whole angelic fringe
on that gorgeous orangish grouse around

CRIPPLED

purple curls ripple the top of the heart
of that decorative olden cabbage inurned

FOND

of sedge-ferns offering along the shore edge shade

ONCE IN FLORENCE

race me to
that bunch
of grapes

ONLY 2 OR 3 ROUTES

only two or three that seem
like true streets through these trees

thumb puzzle

piloting giraffes

SYLVAN STRAND

slight sliver of beeches rejoicing in the moonlight winking

NO CALL TO QUIT THESE FIELDS YET

where silent sword defenses till

BESET BY NOISES

off hailing and baying
with that mouthy snout

STARING AT ASTOUNDING CLATTER

just the sound of a hound descending

FLOWERING DOG WOOD

might be stooping willow

SPRING CRICKETS

bring crocuses astir
as at the sprinklers
when iris open aster
starting in the dusk

JUDO MAT

falling neptune fountain revels

QUAIL DAMAGE

how sad for
those birds

CHATEAU DE VERSAILLES

shadow of a cat over water lithe
-ly padding sanding feeling fine

CHATEAU DE VERSAILLES

elsewhere you would go on lyric wings

CAUGHT BIRDS

four old
eating birds

TWO CROWS OVER THERE

there's a crowd now
growing from them
fielding old seeds

DOVES

dove

DIVERS

different swimmers looking lean
-ing into it the basin brimming
with brief flecking in versions
of letters a-flutter to a light

COCTEAU

l'oiseau chante
avec ses doigts

COCTEAU

unfledged crook-spur waterfowl yell
-owing in the shallows' fallow laps

PHONEPOLES

penelope's

oldpasties

RIVEN WIRES

over some dozen doves dozing does
a wire strung to those poles rove

CAWKING

a flock of chalk-
white aging birds
flew by, coughing
at a watching sky

CRANKY OLD WATERFOWL

complaining about the weather,

disguised by feathered hankies

CAUCUS

because of crows echoing
between the brickwork
cemetery wall & etcetera

COSSACK

riding once over
those windy hills down
looking whilst

WORSE BIRDS

was not

was so

MORE BIRDS

v Brne

ELUSIVE CAUSE

a mote, mute, floats
in a moody votive air

ASPECTS OF PASSING SEED

thou dost speak's

MON COEUR

secretive but curious skulker of dense thickets

AFTERWORD

I *Mote* be *Moightily* Offended (& 'Perturbed'), contact my Solicitor & commence a Cause of Action for (dastardly!) Infringement Upon *My* ('Proprietary') *Form*—HOW DARE CRAIG DWORKIN *Write* (AND PUBLISH !) poems which 'explore' the sorts of title/text relations for which certain of my early works Ought to be *Better Known* ?

Au Contraire, I am Delighted to find these (sometimes 'similar', occasionally 'equal' & often radically *different* (in 'subject matter & tone') accomplished poems . . . *There* . . . in the spaces of their pages (*relating* to each other in space, as what they are & can be, *if* one undertakes to *Read Them*) . . . some are (even/arguably) 'better than mine' !

Why *doesn't* somebody take up Louis Zukofsky's word-count line, & begin to make a real *'Common Measure'* from it—like another/'public' blank verse (remember the form that 'served so well', & forwarded the ('larger'/dramatic/'epic') interests of Shakespeare, Milton, Keats, etc., down to Robt Lowell?) ?

What's *wrong* with our Community of Poets, such that each next 'new one' has to be so studiously/stylistically (*'New'*) *Idiosyncratic* . . . ? (Doesn't that make for an endlessly 'terminal' fragmenting off . . . ?)

In the meantime, these ('lyric') title/text relations are 'right there' to be inquired into (nobody's 'property'—how *banal* it is to insist on 'Originality' in these matters of available form !), by anybody who wants to 'carry on' WCW's, LZ's, Creeley's, my, & Craig Dworkin's example.

Is it all *'Dust'* . . . ?

Why *moight not* the Title/Text Relation (inquired into) yield further knowledge of what it is to be alive in this world, *through this form* ? ?

—Robert Grenier
July 15, 2011

ROOF BOOKS

the best in language since 1976

Titles

- Andrews, Bruce. **Co**. Collaborations with Barbara Cole, Jesse Freeman, Jessica Grim, Yedda Morrison, Kim Rosefield. 104p. $12.95.
- Andrews, Bruce. **Ex Why Zee**. 112p. $10.95.
- Andrews, Bruce. **Getting Ready To Have Been Frightened**. 116p. $7.50.
- Arakawa, Gins, Madeline. **Making Dying Illegal**. 224p. $22.95.
- Benson, Steve. **Blue Book**. Copub. with The Figures. 250p. $12.50
- Bernstein, Charles. **Controlling Interests**. 80p. $11.95.
- Bernstein, Charles. **Islets/Irritations**. 112p. $9.95.
- Bernstein, Charles (editor). **The Politics of Poetic Form**. 246p. $12.95; cloth $21.95.
- Brossard, Nicole. **Picture Theory**. 188p. $11.95.
- Cadiot, Olivier. **Former, Future, Fugitive**. Translated by Cole Swensen. 166p. $13.95.
- Champion, Miles. **Three Bell Zero**. 72p. $10.95.
- Child, Abigail. **Scatter Matrix**. 79p. $9.95.
- Davies, Alan. **Active 24 Hours**. 100p. $5.
- Davies, Alan. **Signage**. 184p. $11.
- Davies, Alan. **Rave**. 64p. $7.95.
- Day, Jean. **A Young Recruit**. 58p. $6.
- Di Palma, Ray. **Motion of the Cypher**. 112p. $10.95.
- Di Palma, Ray. **Raik**. 100p. $9.95.
- Doris, Stacy. **Kildare**. 104p. $9.95.
- Doris, Stacy. **Cheerleader's Guide to the World: Council Book** 88p. $12.95.
- Dreyer, Lynne. **The White Museum**. 80p. $6.
- Dworkin, Craig. **Strand**. 112p. $12.95.
- Dworkin, Craig, editor. **The Consequence of Innovation: 21st Century Poetics**. 304p. $29.95.
- Edwards, Ken. **Good Science**. 80p. $9.95.
- Eigner, Larry. **Areas Lights Heights**. 182p. $12, $22 (cloth).
- Eisenhower, Cathy. **would with and**. 120p. $13.95
- Fitterman, Robert. **Rob the Plagiarist**. 108p. $13.95
- Fodaski, Elizabeth. **Document**. 80p. $13.95
- Gardner, Drew. **Petroleum Hat**. 96p. $12.95.
- Gizzi, Michael. **Continental Harmonies**. 96p. $8.95.
- Gladman, Renee. **A Picture-Feeling**. 72p. $10.95.
- Goldman, Judith. **Vocoder**. 96p. $11.95.
- Gordon, Nada. **Folly**. 128p. $13.95

- Gordon, Nada. Scented Rushes. 104p. $13.95
- Gottlieb, Michael. **Ninety-Six Tears**. 88p. $5.
- Gottlieb, Michael. **Gorgeous Plunge**. 96p. $11.95.
- Gottlieb, Michael. **Lost & Found**. 80p. $11.95.
- Greenwald, Ted. **Jumping the Line**. 120p. $12.95.
- Grenier, Robert. **A Day at the Beach**. 80p. $6.
- Grosman, Ernesto. **The XULReader: An Anthology of Argentine Poetry (1981–1996)**. 167p. $14.95.
- Guest, Barbara. **Dürer in the Window, Reflexions on Art**. Book design by Richard Tuttle. Four color throughout. 80p. $24.95.
- Hills, Henry. **Making Money**. 72p. $7.50. VHS videotape $24.95. Book & tape $29.95.
- Huang Yunte. **SHI: A Radical Reading of Chinese Poetry**. 76p. $9.95
- Hunt, Erica. **Local History**. 80 p. $9.95.
- Kuszai, Joel (editor) **poetics@**, 192 p. $13.95.
- Inman, P. **Criss Cross**. 64 p. $7.95.
- Inman, P. **Red Shift**. 64p. $6.
- Lazer, Hank. **Doublespace**. 192 p. $12.
- Levy, Andrew. **Paper Head Last Lyrics**. 112 p. $11.95.
- Mac Low, Jackson. **Representative Works: 1938–1985**. 360p. $18.95 (cloth).
- Mac Low, Jackson. **Twenties**. 112p. $8.95.
- McMorris, Mark. **The Café at Light**. 112p. $12.95.
- Mohammad, K. Silem. The Front. 104p. $13.95
- Moriarty, Laura. **Rondeaux**. 107p. $8.
- Nasdor, Marc. **Sonnetailia**. 80p. $12.95
- Neilson, Melanie. **Civil Noir**. 96p. $8.95.
- Osman, Jena. **An Essay in Asterisks**. 112p. $12.95.
- Pearson, Ted. **Planetary Gear**. 72p. $8.95.
- Perelman, Bob. **Virtual Reality**. 80p. $9.95.
- Perelman, Bob. **The Future of Memory**. 120p. $14.95.
- Perelman, Bob. **Iflife**. 140p. $13.95.
- Piombino, Nick, **The Boundary of Blur**. 128p. $13.95.
- Price, Larry. **The Quadragene**. 72p. $12.95.
- Prize Budget for Boys, **The Spectacular Vernacular Revue**. 96p. $14.95.
- Raworth, Tom. **Clean & Will-Lit**. 106p. $10.95.
- Reilly, Evelyn. **Styrofoam**. 72p. $12.95.
- Retallack, Joan. Procedural Elegies/Western Civ Cont/. 120p. $14.95.
- Robinson, Kit. **Balance Sheet**. 112p. $11.95.
- Robinson, Kit. **Democracy Boulevard**. 104p. $9.95.
- Robinson, Kit. **Ice Cubes**. 96p. $6.
- Rosenfield, Kim. **Good Morning—MIDNIGHT—**. 112p. $10.95.
- Scalapino, Leslie. **Objects in the Terrifying Tense Longing from Taking Place**. 88p. $9.95.
- Seaton, Peter. **The Son Master**. 64p. $5.
- Shaw, Lytle, editor. **Nineteen Lines: A Drawing Center Writing Anthology**. 336p. $24.95

- Sherry, James. **Popular Fiction**. 84p. $6.
- Silliman, Ron. **The New Sentence**. 200p. $10.
- Silliman, Ron. **N/O**. 112p. $10.95.
- Smith, Rod. **Music or Honesty**. 96p. $12.95
- Smith, Rod. **Protective Immediacy**. 96p. $9.95
- Stefans, Brian Kim. **Free Space Comix**. 96p. $9.95
- Stefans, Brian Kim. **Kluge**. 128p. $13.95
- Sullivan, Gary. **PPL in a Depot**. 104p. $13.95
- Tarkos, Christophe. **Ma Langue est Poétique—Selected Works**. 96p. $12.95.
- Templeton, Fiona. **YOU—The City**. 150p. $11.95.
- Torre, Mónica de la. **Public Domain** 104 p. $13.95.
- Torres, Edwin. **The All-Union Day of the Shock Worker**. 112 p. $10.95.
- Torres, Edwin. **Yes Thing No Thing**. 128 p. $14.95.
- Tysh, Chris. **Cleavage**. 96p. $11.95.
- Vallejo, César. Translated by Joeseph Mulligan. **Against Professional Secrets**. 104 p. $14.95.
- Ward, Diane. **Human Ceiling**. 80p. $8.95.
- Ward, Diane. **Relation**. 64p. $7.50.
- Watson, Craig. **Free Will**. 80p. $9.95.
- Watten, Barrett. **Progress**. 122p. $7.50.
- Weiner, Hannah. **We Speak Silent**. 76 p. $9.95
- Weiner, Hannah. **Page**. 136 p. $12.95
- Wellman, Mac. **Miniature**. 112 p. $12.95
- Wellman, Mac. **Strange Elegies**. 96 p. $12.95
- Wolsak, Lissa. **Pen Chants**. 80p. $9.95.
- Yasusada, Araki. **Doubled Flowering: From the Notebooks of Araki Yasusada**. 272p. $14.95.

ROOF BOOKS are published by
Segue Foundation
300 Bowery • New York, NY 10012
Visit our website at **seguefoundation.com**

ROOF BOOKS are distributed by
SMALL PRESS DISTRIBUTION
1341 Seventh Street • Berkeley, CA. 94710-1403.
Phone orders: 800-869-7553
spdbooks.org